Path of the
Sacred Masculine

Contemplation Tools for Your Journey

KAREN KIESTER

ISBN: 978-0-9909708-0-4

Cover design: James Jarvis
Interior illustrations: Keith Johnson
Interior page design: Jeff Brandenburg

Published by New Dimensions Press
www.pathofthesacredmasculine.com
info@PathoftheSacredMasculine.com

First printing, 2014

Printed in the United States of America

This book and cards are dedicated to the
mothers of sons who abandon stereotypes,
encourage their sons' uniqueness and allow
them to become their true selves.

Contents

➤ THE CARDS ➤

Acknowledgements

First, I want to thank Keith Johnson for bringing the contemplation cards to life with his amazing artistry. I trusted the Universe would provide me with the perfect artist for this project of wisdom and it did in Keith. He created images that capture the essence of each and every card. It was an incredible journey to witness how Keith took the information from the matrix (see Appendices—Matrix) and our conversations to manifest the cards. I shall always remember being introduced to the cards one by one and the deep awe that I felt. They far surpassed anything that I imagined. I am and will be forever grateful to Keith for this precious gift.

Secondly, I want to thank my dear friends, Laurice, Stacey, Felice and my beloved James for their feedback, encouragement and support. And lastly, to Josef, the Earthly Father of the Christ for entrusting me with this undertaking.

May the cards and book speak to your heart and soul and take you to places that you never imaged.

Introduction

At a time when the patriarchy is diminishing and god-
desses abound, what of the sacred masculine? As confusion
about masculinity and what is means "to be a man" seems
to muddy the water further, it is time for a simple yet profound tool to offer some assistance: a contemplation card
deck and guide book.

These cards are a gift from Josef, the earthly father of the
Christ. You know, the Josef and Mary, Josef, betrothed of
Mary, mother of Jesus Christ. That man who clearly played
a major role in the life of an extraordinary being, offering
wisdom and guidance to this child who would grow to be a
man and have a profound effect on the world. Who better
to offer information and guidance about the Sacred Masculine than Josef? To learn about that story and the journey
of the cards and book's creation see the section "Karen's
Story."

To me, Josef truly represents the sacred masculine, and
in working with his gifts (information about the cards) it
became clear to me that it is time to honor the sacred masculine and bring forth information about this "essence"
which has been suppressed. There are many card decks
out there, and I have not found one that honors the sacred
masculine.

The purpose of this book, which supports the contemplation card deck, is to offer the opportunity to reflect upon
and embrace the sacred masculine. It is my hope that the
cards and book will be used to affirm what is wonderful

and needed from the sacred masculine, as well as to offer guidance to broaden ones view of the sacred masculine.

If you are looking for an "answer" book, this is not it! This book and cards are meant to be a guide to help you find your own answers. You are the expert! All of the answers you seek are within you.

The deck is based on a matrix of 9 directions or "suits" modeled after the 8 major compass points plus the center point. It is then cross sectioned by categories consisting of archetypes, tools, elements and realms yielding 36 cards (i.e. 9 directions times 4 categories).

The core premise is that the sacred masculine is energy rather than gender. It is not about having answers, or being the "expert." It is about posing questions that will lead one to self-discovery. It encourages you to question your perceptions and your belief systems and to be open to new possibilities.

The cards and the book can provide insights and guidance. The configuration employs the analogy of the medicine wheel. From any point on the wheel there are supporting factors of the companions, which include the corresponding categories to the left and right and cross points of any given position. All are "influenced" by the center point.

The cards are to be used in conjunction with the book which offers descriptions and ways to embody the card and questions for reflection. The book is aimed towards men, yet women will also find value in its pages and images for we all have both masculine and feminine energy and tendencies. The cards are tools to bring balance into one's life. The cards were created by Keith Johnson, an amazing artist. He is a man who brings his life experience to the images. See "Keith's Process."

Rather than being an authoritative work, this book seeks to plant seeds so that the reader can arrive at his or her own representations. It may seem odd for a woman to derive such information, but my life and personality have provided many "masculine" experiences, which is true for many other women, just the same as when men have "feminine" experiences. To me, this supports the premise that masculine and feminine are "energies" and do not simply describe the body you were born with or your sexual orientation.

How to use these cards/words:

You can work with the cards alone, or the book alone or the cards and book together. Trust how you are drawn to work with them. And it can change. Go with it. Working with the cards is meant to be playful and yet profound. There is no "right way." It is all good.

Let the images and words "speak to you." They offer wisdom and knowledge if you allow yourself to truly listen. As you spend time with the cards and words, see what arises within you. Also pay attention to any blockage or resistance that may occur. Simply note them and give them time to reveal themselves. The information can come in a few minutes, during your morning shower, when working out, while taking a long walk or while meditating. The important consideration is to listen and pay attention to information that is being offered to you. It may come in a dream, during a conversation, even while watching TV. The universe is very resourceful.

Often when our attention is on something else the meaning or insight will "bubble" up to our consciousness. This is an opportunity to deeply listen to the wisdom that exits within all of us. These materials offer an opportunity to extend and balance your point of view, to see things with new eyes, to hear with new ears, and comprehend at a much deeper level.

And at the same time the cards and words can be used in a fun and whimsical way. Wisdom comes in many forms. Often wanting to "get it right" and analyze it to pieces only pushes the information father away. These materials can help you reframe circumstances and stories in your life. Often simply relaxing with "what is" brings significant changes in your perceptions and experiences.

If that overwhelms you, here are a few suggestions:

1. Read through the book, one card at a time. Look at the card. Notice the details in the card. The colors used. Really "drink" in the images. Read the section in the book. Reflect on the words. See what meaning and insights come to you. You can read one each day or move to the next when you feel you have fully embraced the message of the card. You can start at the front of the book, or from the back to the front. Do something different!

2. Or close your eyes and open the book to a page. Find the card and reflect on the image. What is the card conveying to you? Go to the book and read about the card. See if the words match your perceptions. It is fine if they don't. It is about your reflections.

3. Shuffle the cards. Go through the deck one by one. You can do one card a day or move along at the pace that feels comfortable to you. You may stay with one card for a few days and you may do two or three cards in one day. Read the section in the book about the card if you are drawn to one. It is all perfect.

The cards were not designed as a Tarot deck, yet they can be used for readings using any of the various card spreads. That information is readily available on the web or from other sources. It is my intent to keep it simple.

Card Page Layout

The page begins with the name of the card. This is the same name that appears on each card at the bottom. Use this word to go between the cards and the information in this book about the card.

Below the name is the "keyword" for the card. This is a word that describes what the card represents which is followed by a paragraph offering an explanation of the meaning of the card. Use this as a reference or guide to develop your understanding of the card.

The next section is "To Embody." This portion offers ideas that can help you personify the "essence" of the card. This is followed by "Choosing This Card" which provides questions to consider, perhaps giving insights about a card and its subject. At the end are identifying factors about the card: type, direction, suit mates, and companions which consist of "on the right," "on the left," and "across."

A card will be one of four types: Archetype, Element, Tool or Realm.

The Archetypes come in two classifications: relation and role. Relations represent the roles that a man can journey through in his life, (son, brother, father, and grandfather). These cards allow exploration of the relationships a man can experience in his lifetime. Roles afford the opportunity to explore the quintessential aspects of a man's existence (craftsman, lover, nobleman, and warrior). And there is a unique ninth archetype: oneness.

The Elements are air, earth, fire, heavens, magnetic, metal, rock, water, and wood. The elements offer a link to the present time in this three dimensional world. They activate our senses and remind us of our physical presence.

The Realms are animal, divine, earthly, emotional, gnome, mental, spiritual, and vibrational. They are "otherworldly," (i.e., beyond this time and place) and can help take you to the next "level" of awareness and experience in your life.

The Tools are bell, book, chalice, drum, flute, hammer, lyre, mirror, and sword. These are man-made items that can be used in our day-to-day lives. They range from practical to inspirational. They speak to man's intelligence and his desire for beauty.

Each of the types belongs to one of nine directions (the 8 compass points plus the center) thus forming a wheel with spokes. The distinct types that belong to the same direction are "suit mates." For example the southwest has the archetype of father, the tool book, the element rock and the realm of mental. The cards that belong to a given direction are assisted by their suit mates. So the father is aided by books, rocks and mental.

Last are the companions. They are the same types (e.g. archetype) that are to the right, left, and across from a specific type on the wheel. For example the companions of the father are right: lover, left: nobleman, and across: brother. The companion to the right can help clear obstructions and reduce frustrations. The companion to the left can assist in assimilating new information. And the cross companion can help reduce resistance to whatever event or task is in need of assistance.

For example, if the father is feeling frustrated, he can look to the lover to offer ways to reduce his frustrations. If he desires more information he can look to the nobleman to supply that. And if he is experiencing resistance, he can look to the brother for support.

In other words, we are not alone on this journey. There are many ways to receive assistance and support. We only need be aware of all that is around us waiting to provide that support and accept it.

Card Layout

The cards have a general layout that will vary slightly from card to card. The name of the card is printed at the bottom. Use this word to find the write up about the card in this book in the section that follows. The cards are listed alphabetically by name.

On each card you will find a compass-like icon that designates the direction or "suit" of the card. A red line, that is part of the icon, points in the direction of the suit. A red dot in the center of the compass designates the four cards that belong to the "center" direction. Use this symbol to help you gather the four cards belonging to a given "suit" (i.e. archetype, element, realm and tool) if you wish to work with the cards as a directional set.

The type of card is indicated by the following symbols:

Archetype	
Element	
Realm	
Tool	

These symbols will help you gather the 9 cards belonging to a given type. You may also find it helpful to gather the companion cards, listed at the bottom of the card information page, and work with them as a unit, to actually see them in their selected placement. For example, for the Father card, his right companion is the Lover, his left companion is the Nobleman and his across companion is the Brother. Place them before you in that configuration. Sit quietly and allow any insights to arise within you.

And, of course, you are free to mix and match the cards by following your own inner guidance. Try randomly selecting one archetype, one element, one realm and one tool card, then lay them out in front of you side by side and allow your imagination to create a story that interweaves the images.

The possibilities are endless.

.

The Cards

AIR

AIR

Life

Air is a substance that can be felt but cannot be seen. We can see the effects of air like a gentle breeze blowing leaves or a strong wind bending tree branches. Just like our intelligence, we can see the effects of how we use it but we cannot see our mind at work. Air keeps us alive. Air is life. Each in-breath gives us the opportunity to start afresh. Each out-breath allows us the chance to release that which no longer serves us. Air gets things moving and can be as gentle as a summer's breeze or as powerful as a gale. It can be subtle or exhibit great force. Air is felt but not seen. We can see the effects of airflow but air itself remains unseen.

To Embody

Be conscious about your presence. At times be like a gentle summer's breeze: present, but not obvious. At other times make your presence known. Be a force to be reckoned with. Learn when to speak with authority and when to remain silent.

AIR

Choosing this Card

✦ Are there times that you are unseen?

✦ Do you have old wounds that need to be released?

✦ Have you experimented with breath work?

✦ Can you make your presence known in a gentle and subtle way?

✦ Do you long for recognition?

Type:	Element
Direction:	Northwest
Suit Mates:	Grandfather, Emotional, Flute
Companions:	On the right: Earth On the left: Metal Across: Water

Air fill me with life

Expand my presence

Let me soar

Finding my worth

ANIMAL

ANIMAL

Primal

Animal represents our basic primal tribal nature. It is the "core" that drives us to survive and perpetuate (breed). It gives us an appreciation and respect for those animals that help us survive by being our food. And gratitude for those animals that provide companionship as a pet. Animal also represents family groups and communities as that is how many animals survive—by being part of a group. Animal also represents the physical aspect of our being, the ability to move and do tasks with ease and grace.

To Embody

Take care of your body. Enjoy its sensual aspects. Participate in group and/or community activities. Eat healthily and if those foods came from an animal, appreciate the sacrifice of the animal's life so that yours can continue. Spend time in nature and observe animals and how they live.

ANIMAL

Choosing this Card

✦ Are you taking care of your physical self?

✦ Do you recognize and appreciate your unique beauty?

✦ Do you have a community you belong to?

✦ What can you learn from the animals in your life?

✦ Are your relationships with your family healthy and joyful?

Type:	Realm
Direction:	North
Suit Mates:	Warrior, Metal, Sword
Companions:	On the right: Inner
	On the left: Emotional
	Across: Spiritual

The animal in my heart roars

So others can hear me

And know I am here

BELL

BELL

Resonate

A bell can produce a single vibrant tone that reverberates for a long time and slowly fades away. It waits to be struck and then releases a pure sweet tone that can permeate all. It causes a vibration in our body which then fills our whole being. It helps us resonate with life. We can be carried away by the wave of the tone and let it take us where it will. The tone can open our hearts to let our inner and outer beings unite in oneness and be carried forth in the awareness that All is One.

To Embody

Allow yourself to be filled with the beauty that surrounds you. It can be sounds, sights, smells and feelings such as joy. Let it fill the whole of your being and share it with others simply by your presence. Share the experience with others letting it continue to grow and bring joy.

Choosing this Card

↢ Do you have things that bring you joy?

↢ Do you sing and feel the resonance in your body?

↢ Can you find the music in the everyday world?

↢ Do you allow your heart to be opened?

↢ Do you experience oneness?

Type:	Tool
Direction:	Center
Suit Mates:	Oneness, Heavens, Divine
Companions:	all Tools

Sound the bell

Let the tone ring on

As ripples across a pond

Traveling ever more

BOOK

BOOK

Knowledge

A book is the symbol of knowledge. That knowledge can be practical and hold traditions. It can contain sacred truths or an exciting story. A book can be elegantly bound and passed along to others for their enjoyment. It can be for reference or pure enjoyment. It can contain facts or fiction. Most of all it is meant to be shared.

To Embody

Use your knowledge to gain wisdom. Know that sometimes a well-posed question rather than advice is a far superior way to help another gain knowledge and wisdom. Share your knowledge when invited to do so.

BOOK

Choosing this Card

- Do you willingly share what you know with others?

- Do you withhold what you know so that you have an "advantage" over others?

- What role do books play in your life?

- What part do traditions play in your life?

- Do you have traditions that you hold, honor and share with others?

Type:	Tools
Direction:	Southwest
Suit Mates:	Father, Rock, Mental
Companions:	On the right: Chalice On the left: Lyre Across: Drum

A book falls open

To a page

Offering wisdom

Do you feel it?

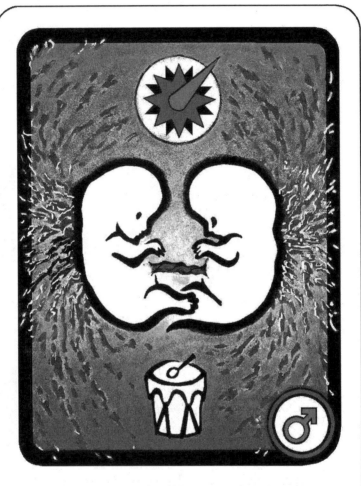

BROTHER

BROTHER

Advocate

The brother is an advocate and friend to all—young, old, male, female, four-leggeds, and winged-ones. He carries a masculine energy without overt sexuality, yet his sexuality is neither repressed nor denied. It is held in a sacred place. His first thought and duty is being of service. Being a helper and/or supporter in whatever form is needed. It can be working alongside community members to complete a task, or watching a group of children play, or feeding an invalid. All these tasks are done with honor, integrity, and duty. The bother enjoys and is fulfilled by the sheer pleasure of helping his community. Yet he takes time for himself and knows his boundaries and when to say "no" to a request.

To Embody

Look for opportunities to be of service for it will bring joy to your life. Appreciate tasks that have a physical component to them. Work with a variety of people and situations and enjoy the richness they bring to your life. Seek your community and become an active member.

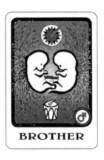

BROTHER

Choosing this Card

↢ Do you volunteer on a regular basis?

↢ Do you live your life with integrity?

↢ Have you created your personal community?

↢ Do you enjoy helping?

↢ Are your boundaries clear?

Type:	Archetype (Relation)
Direction:	Northeast
Suit Mates:	Magnetic, Inner, Drum
Companions:	On the right: Warrior
	On the left: Craftsman
	Across: Father

Oh brother, sweet brother

Always near

Lending a hand

Life is richer

Because of you

CHALICE

CHALICE

Lover of Life

The chalice represents the sacred feminine which is honored and protected by the sacred masculine, honored and held by strong hands as a loving presence. It represents a lover of life. For both feminine and masculine are needed to create human life. The chalice symbolizes a reverence for life in all its forms, and offers the chance to appreciate and acknowledge beauty in all of its manifestations.

To Embody

Treasure the simple elegance of life and all that creation brings. Have creativity be part of your daily life and also respect and enjoy the creativity of others. Learn to see beauty in the most unusual places and aspects of life. Celebrate and share what you find.

CHALICE

Choosing this Card

✦ Are you giving yourself some creative time each day?

✦ Are your creative endeavors nurturing and feeding you?

✦ Do you honor life and revel in all it possibilities?

✦ Do you treasure the women in your life—mother, lover, sisters, daughters and female friends?

✦ Do you see the beauty in all women?

Type:	Tools
Direction:	South
Suit Mates:	Lover, Fire, Spiritual
Companions:	On the right: Mirror On the left: Book Across: Sword

Chalice of the goddess

Full and rich

Shining beauty

Reflecting all

CRAFTSMAN

CRAFTSMAN

Earth Keeper

The craftsman uses his gifts of the earth in a wise way. In balance, he does not deplete resources. He reuses whatever and whenever he can. He is an earth keeper. He does his tasks with the perfect balance of beauty and function, such as building a garden fence of bent branches with a stunning archway at the entrance and bird houses on the fence posts. No matter how mundane a task may seem, it is done as a marriage of beauty and function. He works with his hands and prefers manual tools to electric. He wants to be connected to his project. He lets the materials "talk" to him, like the sculptor who, when sculpting a horse, removes everything that does not look like a horse. He is following his inner guidance.

To Embody

Find and enjoy the beauty that surrounds you. Appreciate the tasks that come your way. Find your inner "'artist" and let it assist in whatever chores you need to do. Share your gifts and allow others to enjoy and appreciate them. Create stunning objects from common materials, especially those that others consider junk.

CRAFTSMAN

Choosing this Card

↞ Do you often work with your hands?

↞ Is beauty a part of whatever you do?

↞ Can you find the purpose in your tasks?

↞ Do you allow beauty to reveal itself in unusual ways and forms?

↞ Are you willing to teach others your skills?

Type:	Archetype (Role)
Direction:	East
Suit Mates:	Wood, Earthly, Hammer
Companions:	On the right: Brother On the left: Son Across: Nobleman

Tinker and ponder

Craft me a gift

To be cherished

As I use it daily

DIVINE

DIVINE

Love

Within each of us there is a place that holds the Divine. It is pure love. Some consider it our soul and our connection point to all creation. It takes us beyond our human form and allows us to know the beauty in all things no matter what we see externally. It is pure unconditional love.

To Embody

Come from a place of unconditional love in your interactions with others. You can often feel this in your heart area. Be compassionate with yourself when this is a struggle. It is a daily practice which starts moment by moment throughout the day until it becomes a habit. Take a deep breath, close your eyes and feel pure love pouring forth from your heart.

DIVINE

Choosing this Card

↞ Do you find yourself judging others?

↞ Do you need to forgive yourself for anything?

↞ Do you love yourself unconditionally?

↞ Are you compassionate when dealing with others?

↞ Do you smile at strangers?

Type:	Realm
Direction:	Center
Suit Mates:	Oneness, Heavens, Bell
Companions:	all Realms

Oh, Divine joy

That fills my

Heart and soul

Reminding me

I always AM

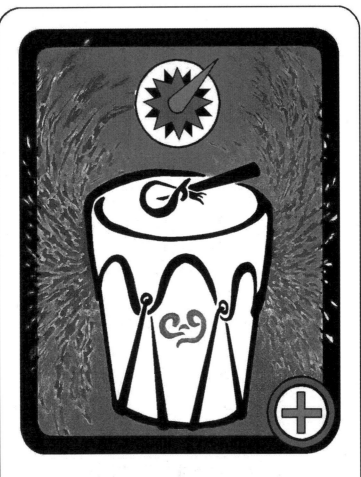

DRUM

DRUM

Earth Pulse

The drum connects us to the mother, to ourselves and to others. The beat is like that of our mother when we were in the womb where we grew close to her heart. It is the earth pulse. It is the same as the beat of mother earth letting us know she is here and ever present with us. Can you hear her heartbeat? If you allow your heart to beat in rhythm with her then all is well. If not, go back to that embryonic state and once again have your heart beat with the rhythm of the earth. Let a drum assist you and let its beat go with you on your journey.

To Embody

Go into nature and sit on the earth until you hear and feel the heartbeat of the earth. Join a drumming circle to create that heartbeat with others and to deeply feel it within yourself. Play a drum in various rhythms and find the affect it has on you. Hold another person and feel their heart beat. Stroke an animal and connect with its heart beat. Experience the oneness and unity it brings.

DRUM

Choosing this Card

- ✦ Are you taking care of your heart physically and emotionally?

- ✦ Do you have a drum which you play on a regular basis?

- ✦ Have you attended a drumming circle and freely participated?

- ✦ Can you feel your heart beat?

- ✦ Do you want to make your own drum?

Type:	Tool
Direction:	Northeast
Suit Mates:	Brother, Magnetic, Inner
Companions:	On the right: Sword
	On the left: Hammer
	Across: Book

Ever constant

Ever beating

My heart is my drum

Calling me home

EARTH

EARTH

Tribal

Earth is the name of our planet and also the dirt we walk upon. We plant in it and often cover it up with concrete and structures. It is the element that truly connects us to this planet and helps us to connect to one another. It is tribal energy is its purest form. It is also the foundation for much of the vegetation that grows on this planet. It is as multidimensional as we are. Some say the earth is also a living breathing being. Care for it as you would a beloved family member.

To Embody

Enjoy the musky smell of a summer's rain on the warm earth. Care for the planet by being aware of the products that you use. Spend time in nature and walk barefoot on the ground. Allow yourself to hear the heartbeat of mother earth.

EARTH

Choosing this Card

✦ Do you recycle all that you can?

✦ Are you a steward for the earth?

✦ Do you enjoy sensuous smells of your body?

✦ Do you garden?

✦ Have you studied permaculture?

Type:	Element
Direction:	West
Suit Mates:	Nobleman, Vibrational, Lyre
Companions:	On the right: Rock On the left: Air Across: Wood

Earth warm and musky

My breath is your breath

Our hearts beat as one

EARTHLY

EARTHLY

Angelic

A plane or level in which caring for the earth is paramount and where one holds a deep devotion for the earth and all of its creatures. This can be done without being physically present. Many who die stay in this realm for a time to help their loved ones grieve and accept their passing. Angels are in this realm.

To Embody

Care for the planet and others as if this could be your last day on earth. Create things of beauty to be remembered by. Do something kind for a stranger. Tell your loved ones how much they mean to you.

EARTHLY

Choosing this Card

↢ Do you believe in angels?

↢ Have you had an experience with otherworldly beings?

↢ How do you want to be remembered?

↢ What is one thing you can do today to make things better for someone?

↢ Do you communicate with your guardian angel?

Type:	Realm
Direction:	East
Suit Mates:	Craftsman, Wood, Hammer
Companions:	On the right: Inner
	On the left: Gnome
	Across: Vibrational

Is that you over my shoulder?

My dear guardian angel

Watching over me

Ever there

EMOTIONAL

EMOTIONAL

Balance

This is a realm that cannot usually be seen yet it can be felt if one is open to it. We can experience the outer expression of emotions, such as tears and loud voices. In the past we have suppressed and hidden our emotions, feeling that they were weak or unnecessary. Yet that has excluded so much from our lives. Emotions are messengers inviting us to look at something that is out of balance within us. They help us find the balance of our body, our mind, and our spirit. Feeling and expressing our emotions brings a richness and fullness to our lives. Know that deep sorrows open us to deep joys.

To Embody

Allow yourself to feel your emotions when they arise and experience the richness they bring. Reflect on what the message of your emotions could be. Let go of the stories that men do not cry. Become a model of realistic emotional expression.

EMOTIONAL

Choosing this Card

- ✦ Do you allow yourself to feel and express your emotions when they arise?

- ✦ Are you compassionate when others cry?

- ✦ Can you support others in healthy expression of their emotions?

- ✦ Do you know the difference between empathy and sympathy?

- ✦ Do you know it is truly a strong man who can show his emotions?

Type:	Realm
Direction:	Northwest
Suit Mates:	Grandfather, Air, Flute
Companions:	**On the right:** Vibrational On the left: Animal Across: Gnome

Joys and sorrows

Pain and grief

Depth of feeling

Emotional me

FATHER

FATHER

Provider

The father is the provider for his family and that of his community. He is a partner to his life mate, offering stability, nurturance and strength. He is the masculine presence in the family, sharing men's ways and men's knowings. It is more than biology that makes one a father. It is the willingness to step into the role; to care for the young and the old and by providing wisdom, substance, guidance, and support to the young and honor, respect, and assistance to the elders.

To Embody

Look for opportunities to support others in their exploration of the role of father. Share your experiences and validate theirs. Offer advice and counsel when it is sought and know often that what is needed is simply to listen and to hold a space within which others are able to hear the answers being provided through their own words.

FATHER

Choosing this Card

✦ What do you need to celebrate and appreciate in your life as a father?

✦ Do you need to heal wounds with your father?

✦ Do you need to heal wounds with your children?

✦ How can you be of service to other fathers?

✦ Now, at this time and in this moment, can you support fatherhood in your life and honor what it means to you?

Type:	Archetype (Relation)
Direction:	Southwest
Suit Mates:	Rock, Mental, Book
Companions:	On the right: Lover On the left: Nobleman Across: Brother

Ever present

Even when not there

Seed of life

Before and forever

FIRE

FIRE

Ardor

Fire is an element that provides many gifts. It gives warmth and light. We use it to cook our food and warm our bodies. It can cause great destruction but can also be used to create things of beauty. It can strengthen metal and turn a clay pot into a stunning piece of porcelain. Its flames can capture our imagination. The coals can represent our ardors and emotions which can be expanded by air and in the end leaves but a small pile of ashes. So like the Phoenix rising, we can become something better.

To Embody

Feel the fires within your body and let them "dance" within you. Let your passions fill your heart and guide you. Let the heat melt your resistance and surrender to insights that arise within you. Let the fires within you crack open that seed which is waiting to be planted to grow.

FIRE

Choosing this Card

✦ How are you destructive in your life?

✦ How do you create beauty?

✦ Are you following your passions?

✦ Are you using your strengths?

✦ Are you radiating who you are to the world?

Type:	Element
Direction:	South
Suit Mates:	Spiritual, Chalice, Lover
Companions:	On the right: Water
	On the left: Rock
	Across: Metal

Flame to embers

Passion expanding

Touching all

Forever more changed

FLUTE

FLUTE

Soul Song

The flute sends its magic through the air like the song of a bird. It tells its story without words, so that the mind can be at rest and the emotions can open and flow with each note. The song can take you to the past to bring a lesson forward to this place and time or it could take you into the future with its immense possibilities. Deeply and gently the sounds stir the memories of the soul. Let your soul sing. Let if reveal its gifts and stories to you.

To Embody

Give yourself a quiet space with enough time to let your soul song emerge. Learn to play a musical instrument. Let your voice express itself through song. Let the tones arise from deep within you and see what insights reveal themselves. Support musicians and song writers.

Choosing this Card

✦ Is music part of your life?

✦ Do you allow music to express what you are feeling?

✦ Can you tell a story without words?

✦ Is there a memory from the past that needs to come forward?

✦ Do you allow yourself to wildly dream of an amazing future?

Type:	Tool
Direction:	Northwest
Suit Mates:	Grandfather, Air, Emotional
Companions:	On the right: Lyre On the left: Sword Across: Mirror

The notes sing

Through the air

Lifting me higher

Watch me soar

GNOME

GNOME

Magic

The gnome is part of the fairy realm, a step beyond this world yet still connected to this earthly plane. He is a wise, mischievous soul who is watchful and helpful. He tends to his business yet he is fully aware of all that is going on around him. Eager to assist when asked, he remains behind the scene making sure that things get handled. He is kind and generous to all persons, things, and animals. He has his own special type of magic.

To Embody

Enjoy nature and all its gifts: trees, water, rocks, plants, and animals. Observe often and "quietly." Help when you can for the pure joy of it, not needing or wanting to be rewarded.

GNOME

Choosing this Card

- ↫ Do you believe in magic?

- ↫ Do you see humor in situations?

- ↫ Do you spend time in nature on a regular basis?

- ↫ Do you have pets that bring joy to your life?

- ↫ In what ways are you generous?

Type:	Realm
Direction:	Southeast
Suit Mates:	Son, Water, Mirror
Companions:	On the right: Earthly
	On the left: Spiritual
	Across: Emotional

A skip and a dance

Merrily strolling by

Enjoying each moment

Looking forward to tomorrow

GRANDFATHER

GRANDFATHER

Wisdom Keeper

The grandfather is the storyteller. His stories contain the customs and traditions of his family and his people, as well as the simplicity of everyday life. His wisdom is part the gift of his age and the depth of understanding of the stories that he tells. He is the wisdom keeper. He adjusts his stories as time and situations warrant. He is the lineage bearer of his family and his people. He is preparing his successors so all will continue in a seamless way. He is quick to forgive with a firm loving hand. Yet he is no one's fool. Those who believe they can trick him are in for a rude awakening which they clearly show that they need. Grandfather's lessons are gentle with a large dose of humor, yet deeply profound and continue to bring forth insights as time passes.

To Embody

Embrace your storyteller and look for opportunities to share your stories. Enjoy the aging process and savor how your life experience have molded your life and helped you become the person that you are now.

GRANDFATHER

Choosing this Card

↞ Do you spend time with your family?

↞ Do you know who your people are?

↞ Have you simplified your life?

↞ Are you loving yet strong?

↞ Do you keep your sense of humor at challenging times?

Type:	Archetype (Relation)
Direction:	Northwest
Suit Mates:	Air, Emotional, Flute
Companions:	On the right: Nobleman
	On the left: Warrior
	Across: Son

Each wrinkle holds a story

Of a fully lived life

Yet the twinkle in his eye

Keeps the secrets

HAMMER

HAMMER

Structure

The hammer shows us we are capable of building structure for ourselves. The structures can be large like a building or a plan for our future or small like a coin box. We can create things to take care of ourselves in many ways and on many levels. Our creativity can manifest many things for us. We can start with raw materials and turn those into whatever we need following a plan, which can be very detailed or simply following our inner guidance. It is about knowing how much force is needed to change something and to use that force to create rather than overpower and destroy it.

To Embody

Create and follow a detailed plan or let your inner guidance direct you. Find the balance between detail and guidance that works for you. It may vary with the task and the group that you are working with. Learn how to show your strength and force to bring structure to a situation and task. At the same time learn to not overpower a situation or person.

HAMMER

Choosing this Card

- ↞ Do you have the right level of structure in your life?

- ↞ Do you know when to follow a detailed plan?

- ↞ Do you know when to follow your inner guidance?

- ↞ Can you see an object and know it can be something else?

- ↞ Do you know when to use force as in a beneficial way?

Type:	Tool
Direction:	East
Suit Mates:	Craftsman, Wood, Earthly
Companions:	On the right: Drum
	On the left: Mirror
	Across: Lyre

Tap, tap, tap

And tap some more

Hear the music

Request an encore

HEAVENS

HEAVENS

Divine Bridge

The heavens are a divine bridge between this place and time and our spiritual world which is timeless. It brings us peace and hope that all will be well and that life has a richness and depth that goes beyond what is on the "surface." This divine bridge allows us to connect with angels and those who have passed, both human and animal.

To Embody

Learn to find a place of peace within you and bring that forward to all you do. Go there when you need to rebalance yourself. Allow yourself to connect with dear friends and family members who have died, including your beloved pets.

HEAVENS

Choosing this Card

↤ Do you wonder what happens after we die?

↤ Do you have a place that soothes you?

↤ Have you made peace with yourself?

↤ Do you have hope for the future?

↤ Do you have a spiritual practice?

Type:	Element
Direction:	Center
Suit Mates:	Oneness, Divine, Bell
Companions:	all Elements

Here and now

There and later

Once before

Ever more

INNER

INNER

Vast Unknown

The Inner is the vast unknown. It is expansive and at the same time held deep within us. It is our connection to the past. It is also a passageway to our future. Our cells hold the memories of our history and of who we are and where we came from. These memories offer insights into why we are here and who we are to become.

To Embody

Spend some time each day in silence and learn to connect, and in time, listen to the vast unknown within you. It can be as simple as five minutes a day. It is not about the amount of time spent. It is about the purity of the connection. It is about taking the time each day and being open to the possibilities. It is not about believing, it is about knowing it is true and allowing that information to surface.

INNER

Choosing this Card

- ✦ Do you wonder what your destiny is?
- ✦ Can you sit in silence for five minutes?
- ✦ Can you find silence in a crowd?
- ✦ Can you be content with "not knowing?"
- ✦ Are there things you just know?

Type:	Realm
Direction:	Northeast
Suit Mates:	Brother, Magnetic, Drum
Companions:	On the right: Animal
	On the left: Earthly
	Across: Mental

Many possibilities

Many probabilities

What will it be?

Ever the questions

LOVER

LOVER

Guardian

The lover is a passionate man who cherishes the sacred feminine and everything female. He is her guardian. Without his skills as a lover the community would perish. He enjoys women and their bodies whatever their shape and size. He aspires to spirituality through sexuality. He knows the pleasures of the body which are held in a sacred space that is filled with honor, integrity, and truth. This is manifested through an exclusive and committed relationship with the woman who speaks to his soul and touches his heart.

To Embody

It is beyond sexual desire. There is a true caring and honoring of the feminine while inviting women to be fully present in that space. It is a sacred trust and understanding of bodily pleasures; and by pleasuring they also receive pleasure from a higher place. They are giving and responsive in a space of reverence and respect. Be passionate and proud, cherishing divine union and all its depths.

LOVER

Choosing this Card

↝ Do you honor and respect women?

↝ Are you caring and loving in your interactions with women?

↝ Do you encourage other men to honor and respect women?

↝ Do you have women friends?

↝ Have you explored Sacred Sexual practices?

Type:	Archetype (Role)
Direction:	South
Suit Mates:	Fire, Spiritual, Chalice
Companions:	On the right: Son
	On the left: Father
	Across: Warrior

Soft and warm

Gentle and bright

Ever evolving

Day turns into night

LYRE

LYRE

Storyteller

The lyre reminds a man to tell his story in a musical way. To share who he is and what he knows in a humorous yet serious way. It is a way to sing his truth like the balladeers and strolling minstrels of old. Let your story reflect your growth and life journey so that others may learn from you and learn more about you.

To Embody

Be creative yet honest in the stories you tell. Let them flow from the place of truth, honor and integrity. Use story to encourage others to reflect and see themselves in the characters. Seek to inspire others with your well-chosen words.

LYRE

Choosing this Card

↩ Does your story change and grow with you?

↩ Do you find music in all that you do?

↩ Can you blend old and new?

↩ Can you find the music in unusual objects?

↩ Can you feel music in the air?

Type:	Tool
Direction:	West
Suit Mates:	Nobleman, Earth, Vibrational
Companions:	On the right: Book
	On the left: Flute
	Across: Hammer

Strumming fingers

Pure tones arise

Filling the air

Words do not matter

MAGNETIC

MAGNETIC

Duality

Something that is magnetic can attract or repel depending on how the objects are positioned. It is a duality. This can be a metaphor for how you interact with people in your life. The attraction or repulsion can be strong or mild. It can be something you are consciously aware of or can happen without your knowledge. It can be something that you sense more than you consciously understand. Opposites can and do attract.

To Embody

Appreciate differing points of view. Try new things that are opposite of what you would normally do and see what you discover. Find people you are drawn to and explore that attraction. Reflect on situations where a slight change brought harmony.

MAGNETIC

Choosing this Card

- ✦ Can you hear differing points of view and find their merits?

- ✦ Are you drawing people that enrich your life?

- ✦ Can you find harmony in unusual situations?

- ✦ Are you pushing away people who can be of assistance to you?

- ✦ How much opposition is in your life?

Type:	Element
Direction:	Northeast
Suit Mates:	Brother, Inner, Drum
Companions:	On the right: Metal
	On the left: Wood
	Across: Rock

The poles align

And then shift

Spinning the world wildly

On a new course

MENTAL

MENTAL

Intellect

Mentality has its place in a balanced person and world. Our mind is an instrument for research. Our minds are very powerful. Yet our minds are not meant to govern us. In certain situations having thought through and created structure and order are of great value. It is about using that information as guidance rather than as a driving force. It is about creating plans that are flexible rather than rigid, plans that can be adapted as new information becomes available. It is also about effectively using logic and our intellect when a situation calls for it, but at the same time not overruling what our hearts and our "guts" tell us.

To Embody

Use your intelligence for the greater good. Read and research to gain information and to be as well informed as you can. Be clear and thorough in your communications when you share information and share it without an "agenda." Use deductive reasoning when it is needed.

MENTAL

Choosing this Card

↞ Is there a subject that you want to study or research?

↞ Are you balancing work and play?

↞ Are you being present or do you get lost in your thoughts?

↞ What does your gut say?

↞ Are your belief systems serving you?

Type:	Realm
Direction:	Southwest
Suit Mates:	Book, Father, Rock
Companions:	On the right: Spiritual
	On the left: Vibrational
	Across: Inner

Will one more piece

Of information help

Or bring more confusion?

METAL

METAL

Strength

Metal takes a journey through extreme heat to evolve to its final form. Often a tool or implement that is durable and strong; sometimes a weapon. It can also be forged into gates and fences and things of beauty. It is resilient and unbending and can last a long time if well-cared for but, if neglected, it rusts and, in time, returns to the earth.

To Embody

Metal can be practical or protective or beautiful. Use your strength for the highest good of all. Know there are times to be firm in what you belief and hold to be true, yet take time to question your beliefs. If fear or resistance arises there is more for you to consider. As a tool, be of service, with your strengths and abilities.

METAL

Choosing this Card

↤ Is your strength being called upon?

↤ Are you being unbending when flexibility is needed?

↤ Are there things that need your protection?

↤ Do you feel you have "walked through the fire?"

↤ Is more practicality needed in your life?

Type:	Element
Direction:	North
Suit Mates:	Animal, Sword, Warrior
Companions:	On the right: Air On the left: Magnetic Across: Fire

Strong and straight

Ridge and present

Watching vigilantly

MIRROR

MIRROR

Reflection

The mirror gives us a reflection of ourselves yet it is a reversed image, so look carefully. There can be distortions in the mirror. Make sure you are truly looking with awareness so that what you see has an element of truth in it. Know your reflection begins within you. We are often a mirror for others which can be challenging, for often the other does not want to see what we are showing them. The same way that others sometimes reveal truths to us which we do not wish to see. Often the most obvious is the most difficult to see without judgment or criticism.

To Embody

Be a mirror for others with compassion and grace. Do not demand that the other see you and acknowledge the message you bring. The more neutral you are the more likely it is that the message will be received. And if another is reflecting to you, receive the message with openness and give it time to reveal itself. If you find yourself in resistance, take note and come back to the information later.

MIRROR

Choosing this Card

↝ Are you hiding something from yourself?

↝ Is the reflection for yourself?

↝ Is the reflection for another?

↝ Can you see what is wonderful?

↝ Is there something you do not wish to see?

Type:	Tool
Direction:	Southeast
Suit Mates:	Son, Water, Gnome
Companions:	On the right: Hammer On the left: Chalice Across: Flute

Mirror mirror

On the tree

Show me what is

Deep inside me

NOBLEMAN

NOBLEMAN

Overseer

The Nobleman is the overseer of the land and of the community. He is a benevolent ruler, keeping things in balance, making sure all are provided for. All community members are honored and respected for their unique talents. All members of the community are allowed to contribute in ways appropriate to their gifts and skills. The land is also well cared for and nourished so it abundantly produces and is not depleted. Animals are treated with care and appreciation. Water is sacred. It is recognized for the life it holds and the life that it brings. There is enough for all. At the core is the nobleman. His inner balance and knowing enable him to oversee the community and land with love and respect and with a loving strength.

To Embody

A true Nobleman is confident yet humble. He offers a firm yet gentle leadership and is loving, kind and appreciative of those he serves. Yet he is no ones fool and does not hesitate to step in a take charge when those rare moments arrive. He can be decisive and firm when needed and accepts responsibility for his actions and decisions. He fully understands he is of service and does not dominate others. He is a part of the whole. He is fulfilling his destiny.

NOBLEMAN

Choosing this Card

✦ Are you a strong yet gentle leader?

✦ Do you acknowledge and support gifts you see in others?

✦ Do you appreciate diversity?

✦ Are you confident yet not over bearing?

✦ Are you a vibrant and vital part of the whole?

Type:	Archetype (Role)
Direction:	West
Suit Mates:	Earth, Vibrational, Lyre
Companions:	On the right: Father
	On the left: Grandfather
	Across: Craftsman

Ever strong

Ever kind

Ever present

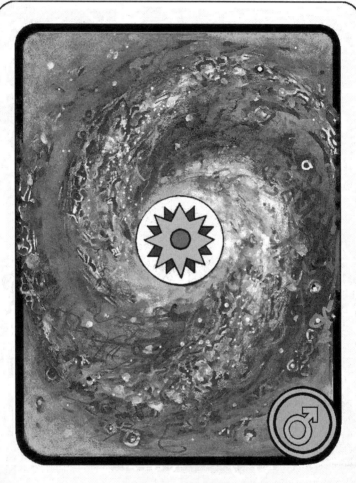

ONENESS

ONENESS

All That IS

This is not about dogma but a consciousness. It is the essence of who we are. It is the nucleus of our world. It is a way of being rather than rules, regulation, and restrictions. It is the Divine presence which is in each and every one of us. It is held in our soul in the vehicle we know as our bodies. It is self-acceptance, joy, and love. It connects us all. We are not alone. It is all that is.

To Embody

Learn to connect with the Divine within. This could be through a meditation or mindfulness practice or even in long-distance running. Discover what it is for you. Learn to see the Divine in others and acknowledge it. The acknowledgement can be silent, simply soul to soul.

ONENESS

Choosing this Card

↜ Can you feel the Divine within you?

↜ Can you sense the Divine in others?

↜ Do you have an active meditation practice?

↜ Do you love and accept yourself?

↜ Do you have joy in your life?

Type:	Archetype
Direction:	Center
Suit Mates:	Heavens, Divine, Bell
Companions:	All Archetypes

Unity

Together

Connection

Wholeness

ROCK

ROCK

Majestic

Rocks are ancient forms which may vary from mountain ranges to pebbles on the beach. As a mountain range they seem to silently observe all that is around them, with their majestic presence, quietly listening and keeping their observations to themselves. They are very slow to erode and change. It takes a great force to break it apart which can be an explosion or the steady forces of nature. Over time its rough surface will be smoothed by water. It can be a striking mountain range or with the patient skill of a sculptor transformed into a thing of beautiful that will last for ages. In its purest form it is a gemstone which is stunningly brilliant and remarkably strong. Rock surfaces vary from ragged to smooth with an endless range of colors. Rocks can be transformed into a functional structure like a retaining wall or into a thing of beauty and elegance like a water fountain. It is a versatile element that can be used for buildings or be crushed for roads.

To Embody

Feel the strength and silence of the rocks within your heart. Allow those feelings to give you strength. Let your presence speak volumes for you without uttering a word. Be aware of those things around you that try to affect you. Know that deep within gemstones are present and more are forming.

ROCK

Choosing this Card

↞ What elements of the rock would be helpful in your life?

↞ Are you being called to stillness?

↞ Is it time to listen?

↞ Is it time to observe?

↞ Do you have a monumental challenge before you?

Type:	Element
Direction:	Southwest
Suit Mates:	Mental, Book, Father
Companions:	On the right: Fire
	On the left: Earth
	Across: Magnetic

Solid

Steadfast

Silent

Brilliant

SON

SON

The Future

The son is the future bringing new ideas with the optimism and enthusiasm of youth. He is full of ideas and bright new inventions that can make life smoother and richer. He has youth, excitement, and boundless energy. He represents our future, the next generation. Let us teach him to leave the world a better place, to think of future generations. Let us instill in him a respect for true elders and to seek their wisdom and council. Let us nurture him to be the change that is needed in the world, in his community, and in his family. Let us share with him those traditions and practices that are worth keeping and encourage him to create new ones that are needed.

To Embody

Let your exuberance shine through. Follow your dreams and bring your ideas to fruition. Keep the wisdoms and knowledge that you held before birth and carried forward with you into this lifetime. Learn to respectfully disagree. Hold onto what you know is true for you and at the same time honor the opinions of others. Look to collaborate and co-create. Do not wait for "tomorrow." Do it today!

SON

Choosing this Card

↰ Are you in touch with your youthful self?

↰ Do you have an elder in your life and do you seek their wisdom?

↰ Are you being inventive?

↰ Do you know how to balance old and new?

↰ What are you enthusiastic about?

Type:	Archetype (Relation)
Direction:	Southeast
Suit Mates:	Water, Gnome, Mirror
Companions:	On the right: Craftsman
	On the left: Lover
	Across: Grandfather

Growing before my eyes

Bringing who you are

To the world

Welcome!

SPIRITUAL

SPIRITUAL

Divine Within

Being spiritual is having a connection to the Divine within. It manifests itself in many ways and forms. It goes beyond belief and is often a matter of faith and trust in that which is beyond ourselves. It evokes compassion and a peaceful state of being. Those who truly embrace a spiritual essence radiate joy and love to their surroundings, and hold a deep knowing that there is a loving presence that guides and protects us all.

To Embody

Find that place within yourself that "holds" your Divine essence. If it is vague, simply begin to acknowledge it and it will make itself known to you. This may take time, be patient. It is often described as a deep "burning" within. Come from a place of humility and confidence in all that you say and do. Be a beacon of peace and serenity. See the Divine in others, no matter how challenging it may be, for if you can reflect it to them, they may begin to know it within themselves.

SPIRITUAL

Choosing this Card

↫ Do you feel a connection to the Divine within you?

↫ Do you sense the presence of the Divine within others?

↫ Do you embrace your divinity and your humanness?

↫ Do you sense the Divine in the earth itself?

↫ Do you feel the Divine within animals and plants?

Type:	Element
Direction:	South
Suit Mates:	Chalice, Lover, Fire
Companions:	On the right: Gnome
	On the left: Mental
	Across: Animal

Radiant heart

Loving presence

True friend

SWORD

SWORD

Protection

The sword provides protection. Its presence can be all that is needed. Hand crafted and elegant, it serves its purpose yet is often a thing of beauty. Created by a combination of the elements from the earth and fire and then hardened with water, it is made with skill and knowledge and has a fine edge. Know when to swiftly use your sword to slice through to the truth, and when to simply have your sword at your side.

To Embody

Know when to hold silence and when to speak. Know where your edge lies. Offer your protection when you feel it is needed, yet do not force it. Be strong yet flexible. Find and appreciate the beauty in all things.

SWORD

Choosing this Card

↢ Is your protection needed?

↢ Is your protection wanted?

↢ Are you too edgy?

↢ Do you use silence to convey the "unspoken"?

↢ Is there a balance of function and beauty in your life?

Type:	Tool
Direction:	North
Suit Mates:	Warrior, Metal, Animal
Companions:	On the right: Drum On the left: Flute Across: Chalice

Cold steel

Sharp point

Swift movement

Sacred companion

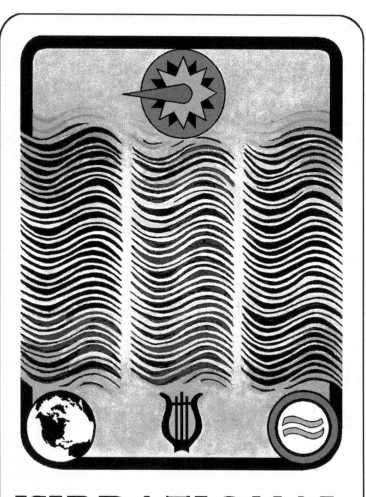

VIBRATIONAL

VIBRATIONAL

Healing Touch

This is part of our world, which in the past, was denied. It is subtle and not "seen" yet it can be felt. It is all around us, for it is how sounds travel through the air and reach our ears. It is another realm which is part of our everyday world. It is also part of loving, healing touch, that connection that begins before the touch is physical. It can be an exciting energy that is in the air or the first warning of danger. It carries healing energies.

To Embody

Be open to feeling the vibrations in our world. Sit quietly and allow yourself to feel them around you. Allow yourself to experience the richness they add to your world. Receive a Reiki or Healing Touch session. Perhaps learn an energetic healing modality.

VIBRATIONAL

Choosing this Card

☙ Can you feel subtle energies?

☙ Do you freely give hugs when welcome?

☙ Do you have a gentle touch?

☙ Do you give yourself some quiet time each day?

☙ Do you sit quietly with a dear friend and hold hands?

Type:	Realm
Direction:	West
Suit Mates:	Nobleman, Earth, Lyre
Companions:	On the right: Mental
	On the left: Emotional
	Across: Earthly

Pulse within pulse

Ever moving

Senses alert

WARRIOR

WARRIOR

Protector

The warrior is the protector of the tribe. Along with his brother warriors he is often in solitude, keeping an outpost, yet he knows his fellow warriors are nearby and will lend support if called. Very in tune to his environment, the warrior senses when things have changed. When something is out of place or when there is a stirring in the air. His physical presence and strength is noticeable and that is often all that is needed to maintain order. He carries fierceness, yet has a gentle heart and is a sensitive being. He can help someone with great tenderness and in a moment switch to a defensive mode. Never first to attack, yet never caught off guard he needs rest to maintain his vigilance and must learn to release his duties to other warriors so he can maintain his strength and alertness.

To Embody

Have strength and confidence and be keenly aware of your surroundings and ready to be of service when called. Someone who truly listens and can hear "in-between" the words that are being spoken. Carry a presence that brings calm and order to a situation.

WARRIOR

Choosing this Card

↤ Are you taking time to rest?

↤ Can you delegate tasks when needed?

↤ Do your follow your heart rather than your head?

↤ Has someone violated your boundaries?

↤ Can you be strong yet not overbearing?

Type:	Archetype (Role)
Direction:	North
Suit Mates:	Metal, Animal, Sword
Companions:	On the right: Brother
	On the left: Grandfather
	Across: Lover

Ever present

Ever knowing

Swift and silent

Core of my being

WATER

WATER

Wholeness

We need water for our survival. We can live weeks without food but can last only a few days without water. Metaphysically water represents our emotional body. Just as water flows so should our emotions. Being emotionally balanced keeps us whole. Know that emotions are a messenger letting us know that something is out of balance. Emotions are neither good nor bad positive nor negative, they are simply messengers.

To Embody

Allow your emotions to flow freely and appropriately. Learn to listen to your emotions and understand what they are trying to tell you. Spend time by bodies of water being soothed by the ebb and flow of the water.

WATER

Choosing this Card

↵ Are you flowing with your life?

↵ Are you appropriately expressing your emotions?

↵ Do you have an unresolved emotional issue?

↵ Do you spend time by a body of water?

↵ Do you value water as an important resource?

Type:	Element
Direction:	Southeast
Suit Mates:	Son, Gnome, Mirror
Companions:	On the right: Wood
	On the left: Fire
	Across: Air

Warm and soothing

Cold and invigorating

Silent and still

Flowing and turbulent

WOOD

WOOD

Fervor

Wood can be used to create things of beauty that are artistic and functional. The woodworker shares his fervor with his creations. It can also be used to build shelters to protect us from the elements or burned to heat our homes, cook our food and help transform other items into things of splendor such as clay to pottery or metal into tools.

To Embody

Appreciate both beauty and functionality; do not sacrifice one for the other. Both can coexist. Find ways to transform your life. Keep learning and growing in all you do. Provide a "safe haven" for friends and family.

Choosing this Card

- Can you create items that are both artistic and functional?
- Do you use your imagination to think outside the box?
- What are ways that you can transform your life?
- Are you multifaceted in what you do?
- Are you a solid and reliable person?

Type: Element

Direction: East

Suit Mates: Craftsman, Earthly, Hammer

Companions: On the right: Magnetic
On the left: Water
Across: Earth

Beauty and function

Artistic and practical

Solid and reliable

Keith's Process

When Karen approached me with her concept of the Sacred Masculine I became fascinated about the implications of such a project. Not only the challenge it would present to myself as an artist, but also to myself as a man. The emergence of the power of women to strike down the prejudices of male dominated societies always struck a sympathetic chord with me, but it also made me aware of how the male has also been cornered into social role-playing and the limitations that that has placed on the Masculine potential.

At first I thought that all I had to do was come up with some illustrations, but the more I became involved with the matrix presented by Josef, the more complex and challenging it became. Two years later I arrived at a completion of the images. I shall always be grateful to Karen for the opportunity to journey within myself and for her patience.

I hope the icons I arrived at will also help others gain insights within themselves.

We all accumulate toxins; some are from our genes, some from our families and some from our societies and schooling. It is the contented person who is able to recognize that which cripples them on their journey toward happiness and to take whatever steps they need to diminish that power over their lives. The Path of Sacred Masculine Contemplation Card Deck is one of many tools to help you on that journey.

I began the images by meditation and drawing ideas and then more meditation trying to weed out the superfluous.

When, after a passage of time, I had arrived at the concept which felt "right." I then cut a linotype of that image. After that came the colors, some dictated by Josef and some from my own inspiration. These were scanned into the computer where I added the symbols and refined and changed them, over and over again, until the image became shining and stopped.

The secret to the creative process is in the word "process."

I could easily begin again and spend a couple more years, but there comes a time when one has to let their children go out into the world to live their own lives. My hope is that you can gain from them the insights that I received from knowing them.

Enjoy,

—Keith Johnson

Karen's Story

A few years back, I was blessed to find myself on "sabbatical" after being laid off from a corporate job. I had the leisure of uncommitted days where I could ponder and reflect. During that time I attended a healing prayer service. That night after the service I had a dream about Josef, the Earthly Father of the Christ, which is the name I know him by. You know, the Josef and Mary Josef. I was puzzled by the dream and it stuck with me. Weeks later I "saw" a biblical dressed male figure in my living room. Needless to say, that was unsettling and I told the figure to leave, which he did.

A few days later the figure was once again in my living room. This time I asked him who he was and why he was there. He replied he was Josef and wanted to talk to me. I told him that having him appear to me was very unsettling but he could "talk" to me in my head and I would listen. So started my re-connection with Josef because after a few days I remembered that I was fascinated by Josef as a child, at that time (and now) I was puzzled that he was seldom spoken of. When I asked questions about him the response was that he was not important. Yet I knew, in my heart of hearts, that he was a vitally important person in the life of the Christ child and man and that Josef taught Christ a great deal and truly "fathered" him. It turned out that Josef had information that he wanted to share and it evolved into the sacred masculine cards and book. I also received information about his life that at some point in the future will become a novel.

The information for the cards was given to me over time, generally during my morning meditation. The cards "aligned" with the eight compass directions and the center point. This had a "rightness" to it and formed its own medicine wheel. The connection to First Nation and Celtic traditions was not lost on me. I took a large piece of poster board and wrote the names of the eight compass directions on the wheel and the center point.

First, I was given the archetypes. Usually within each category (i.e. archetypes, elements, realms and tools) I would receive most of the names and then it would take a few days for the names to finalize. I put these names on 3 by 5 index cards. Most cards would quickly and easily align with a direction that I noted on the card. A few took time. I found if I tried to "help" the process or tried to pick a direction I felt was correct, I would sense that I should not interfere and that the information would come to me in time. It was truly a lesson in surrendering, listening, and staying in touch with my discernment.

When a category was complete, meaning the cards had aligned with all nine direction points, I would move on to the next category. And the process would begin again. As I was creating the cards I kept track of the information in a matrix which is in the Appendices.

It was interesting to me that the cards started in the west which in the Celtic tradition is water and healing. The nobleman came through first and clearly belonged in the west. I find that interesting because we live in a time when "noblemen" are greatly needed. The leadership systems of the globe are greatly in need of healing and need men and women of honor and integrity who will truly represent the people that they serve rather than their own interests. Leaders who respect and honor the diversity of their constituents, be it age, gender, cultural, spiritual, family arrangements, and/or something else.

Then the wheel "traveled" to the northwest, north, etc. which to me indicates first moving into the darkness and then the light. My prior work with medicine wheels was that the wheel started in the east, as the sun arises, then moving southeast, and so on. I have no explanation for this other than this the way the information was given to me. I did question it and was clearly "told" to begin in the west and move north. And so I followed those directions.

As the information for the cards was being given to me, I knew they were destined to become a deck of cards. For a while I was uncertain about the number of cards the deck would comprise of. I did clearly know it was not going to be a Tarot deck. I had ideas about "action" cards and then came to know it would simply be images for the 36 cells of the matrix (i.e. four categories times nine directions).

Also, at first I referred to the deck as a "divination" deck and over time came to know it was a "contemplation" deck. In part, because of the information about each card that was emerging. Additionally, I had been given a "contemplation" by Josef that appears in the Appendices.

I clearly knew that the cards would be created by a male artist, and that it was not my task to complete. The words for the book would be my task. I then began the search for the artist. At first I thought it might be a young man who was moving into manhood sensing that they might bring an interesting perspective as they traveled through that journey in their life. I lived in a university town and considered posting a flier in the art department. Yet I never felt drawn to do that. I had begun to share with friends my experiences with Josef and the card deck project and my desire to find an artist for the project.

At the time I was on the board for a startup non-profit and Keith Johnson was also a board member. At one meeting I shared my Josef experiences and shared my vision of the book and contemplation card deck. I received heartwarming support and enthusiasm for the project. And finally it came to me to ask Keith if he would be interested in being the artist. Gratefully he was and we began a limited series of meetings and discussions. I had a clear sense to give Keith limited information so that the deck could emerge from him and his life experiences. And as I got to know Keith, I knew he was the artist for the project.

It was an amazing and deeply touching experience to meet with Keith as he shared the images he was creating (you can read about Keith's journey in section "Keith's Process"). I was often moved to tears as he shared the card images with me. They were beyond anything I had envisioned and hold such "rightfulness."

So with heart felt conviction, confidence and humility I share with you the Sacred Masculine Contemplation Deck and book. May it truly touch your heart and soul and bring your deep knowing to the surface to enrich your life and that of those around you.

As a disciple and scribe for Josef, the Earthly Father of the Christ, I humbly share this gift with you.

Blessings,

—Karen M Kiester

Appendices

Resources

Advanced Celtic Shamanism, by DJ Conway, The Crossing Press, 2000.

Animal Spirit Guides, by Steven D Farmer, PhD, Hay House, 2006.

Animal-Speak, by Ted Andrews, Llewellyn, 1993.

Archetypal Reiki, by Dorothy May, Journey Editions, 2000.

Emotional Genius, by Karla McLaren, Laughing Tree Press, 2001.

Feng Shui, Arranging Your Home to Change Your Life, by Kirsten M Lagatree, Villard Books 1996.

Fire in the Belly, on Being a Man, by Sam Keen, Bantam Books, 1991.

Follow the Yellow Brick Road, by Richard Saul Wurman, Bantam Books, 1992.

In the Shadow of the Shaman, by Amber Wolfe, Llewellyn, 1988.

Iron John, A Book About Men, by Robert Bly, Vintage Books, 1990.

Man and His Symbols, by Carl G Jung, Doubleday and Company, Inc, 1964.

The Alphabet versus the Goddess, by Leonard Shlain, Penguin Compass, 1998.

The Five Secrets You Must Discover Before You Die, by John Izzo, PhD, Berret-Koehler Publishers, 2008.

The Goddess Oracle, A Way To Wholeness Through Goddess and Ritual, by Amy Sophia Marashinsky, Element, 1997.

The I Ching Workbook, by RL Wing, Doubleday and Company, Inc, 1979.

The Medicine Wheel Garden, Creating Sacred Space for Healing, Celebration, and Tranquility, by E. Barrie Kavasch, Bantam Books, 2002.

The Wisdom of the Crowd, by James Surowiecki, Anchor Books, 2004.

Transference Healing Animal Magic, by Alexis Cartwright, Keeper of the Crystals, 2005.

Matrix

Direction	Archetypes	Elements	Realms	Tools
West	Nobleman	Earth	Vibrational	Lyre
Keyword:	Overseer	Tribal	Healing Touch	Storyteller
Northwest	Grandfather	Air	Emotional	Flute
Keyword:	Wisdom Keeper	Life	Balance	Soul Song
North	Warrior	Metal	Animal	Sword
Keyword:	Protector	Strength	Primal	Protection
Northeast	Brother	Magnetic	Inner	Drum
Keyword:	Advocate	Duality	Vast Unknown	Earth Pulse
East	Craftsman	Wood	Earthly	Hammer
Keyword:	Earth Keeper	Fervor	Angelic	Structure
Southeast	Son	Water	Gnome	Mirror
Keyword:	The Future	Wholeness	Magic	Reflection
South	Lover	Fire	Spiritual	Chalice
Keyword:	Guardian	Ardor	Divine Within	Lover of Life
Southwest	Father	Rock	Mental	Book
Keyword:	Provider	Majesty	Intellect	Knowledge
Center	Oneness	Heavens	Divine	Bell
Keyword:	All That Is	Divine Bridge	Love	Resonate

THE CONTEMPLATION

from Josef,

the Earthly Father of the Christ

As the sacred feminine has been repressed

So, too, has the sacred masculine

When men hold their "sweet boys"

in their hearts

And women are truly "sisters"

The world will BE

Check Out Our Web Site

www.PathoftheSacredMasculine.com

When can I purchase the contemplation cards?

Sign up to be notified when the cards
are available for purchase at:

www.PathoftheSacredMasculine.com/sign-up

At some point in the not too distant future (whatever that
winds up being) look for a novel about the life of Josef, the
Earthly Father of the Christ. It's time to know his story.

And a Related Web Site

JosefSpeaks.com

22113293R00097

Printed in Great Britain
by Amazon